DRUGS AND CODEPENDENCY

Drug addiction can destroy a family by making its members codependents.

THE DRUG ABUSE PREVENTION LIBRARY

DRUGS AND CODEPENDENCY

Mary Price Lee and Richard S. Lee

THE ROSEN PUBLISHING GROUP, INC.
NEW YORK

To
Jan and George Parrish
and
Joan and Stan Henkels
For All the Years of Friendship

Published in 1995 by The Rosen Publishing Group, Inc.
29 East 21st Street, New York, NY 10010

First Edition

Library of Congress Cataloging-in-Publication Data

Lee, Mary Price.
    Drugs and codependency / Mary Price Lee and
Richard S. Lee.
        p.   cm. — (The drug abuse prevention library)
    Includes bibliographical references and index.
    ISBN 0-8239-2065-8
    1. Codependency—Juvenile literature.
    2. Addicts—Family relationships—Juvenile literature.
    3. Children of alcoholics—Juvenile literature.
    4. Children of narcotic addicts—Juvenile literature.
    [1. Codependency.   2. Drug abuse.]   I. Lee,
Richard S. (Richard Sandoval), 1927–   . II. Title.
III. Series.
    RC569.5.C63L44   1995
    616.869—dc20   94-35234
                                                                CIP
                                                                AC

Manufactured in the United States of America

15.95

Contents

Introduction 6

Chapter 1   What Is Codependency? 9

Chapter 2   How does Compulsion Create
            Codependency? 24

Chapter 3   What Codependency Can Do
            to You 35

Chapter 4   How to Start Your Life Over 44

Glossary—*Explaining New Words* 58

Help List 60

For Further Reading 62

Index 63

Introduction

A healthy family works to fulfill each of its member's basic needs. These include love, respect, safety, security, a sense of belonging, self-esteem, and the skills to live independently someday. Each member is responsible for his or her own actions, but the family works together to be happy and healthy.

Families that do not fulfill the needs listed above are not working properly. They are called *dysfunctional*. A dysfunctional family is not a healthy one.

In a dysfunctional family, things are always going wrong. Often, one family member is the cause. The other family members may develop unhealthy ways of coping with the troubles caused by the one member. These unhealthy ways are called *codependency*. The family members who cope in these ways are codependents.

There are many codependent habits. All are bad for the codependent. What is worse, *codependency does not help the family member causing the problem*. But the codependent cannot believe this. He or she stays codependent, trying to solve the problem.

This book will help you to see if you are a codependent. It will show how drug use can cause codependency. It will show what codependency can do to you. If you are a codependent, you will learn how to get the help you need and to live more peacefully with yourself.

In a codependent family, the drug addict or alcoholic
is actually in control.

CHAPTER 1

What Is Codependency?

In her book *Codependent No More*, Melody Beattie, once a codependent and now a writer on the subject, defines codependency. In shorter words, it is this:

You are codependent if you let someone else's wrong actions affect your life so that you feel you *must control the bad things that person does.*

Co-Dependents Anonymous, a self-help group, says that codependents are "people who have trouble with relationships."

Codependents try to take control. But they are also controlled. The family member with the problem often forces the

9

10 others to change the ways they behave. The troublemaker actually controls *them*.

Many codependents come to believe that any problem in the family (and often outside it) is *their* fault. Because they believe this, they try to control what others do and how others behave. They think that controlling others—especially the person with the problem—will make everything all right.

How Codependency Develops

The family situations that can cause you to become a codependent don't arise overnight. But they can arise when the balance of a family is upset. They almost always happen in dysfunctional families. Such families were never balanced to start with.

One or more of these things can cause the balance to become upset—but *only* if the family members can't cope with the situation:

- Drug or alcohol abuse
- Illness or death
- Divorce or remarriage

Adjusting to a death or to living with someone who has a chronic illness can be

Codependency has many possible causes, most of which can destroy a relatively healthy family.

12 hard. Everyone in the family must share the problem and work out the answer.

Losing a job or moving to a new town can be tough, but the healthy family pulls together and survives. Except for chronic illness, these are temporary setbacks for the healthy family. When someone will always need special care, the family plans ways to provide it and still live as happily as they can. The balanced family survives bad times as a *family*. They talk and act together and do not allow problems to unbalance them for long.

Codependency sneaks in when the family is not strong enough to keep or regain its balance or is dysfunctional to begin with. In such families, one member causes problems that affect everyone. Addiction is often the reason. Drug and alcohol abuse are a major cause of addiction.

In marriage, maybe one partner had a alcohol or drug addiction that was hidden when the couple began dating. Or perhaps the problem developed later on in life, after the couple was married. The problem might also exist with a child in the family.

The point is that the addiction is there. Everybody in the family is affected.

The following things are even more difficult for a family to manage, and often

Addictions run from drugs to gambling to overeating.

result in codependency. They are *not* temporary.

- **Addiction** to alcohol or drugs, to dieting or overeating, gambling or excessive spending.
- **Money problems**, often caused or aggravated by one family member's addictive behavior.

Addiction Is a Compulsion

A *compulsion* is the inability to stop a particular behavior. Addiction is a compulsion. The addict believes he or she *is* in control and will not admit there is a

An addictive-compulsive person does not see that he or she has a problem.

problem. If you hear these phrases, you know you are dealing with an addictive-compulsive person:

"I can handle my (drinking, drugs) without your help."

"I can stop (one of the above) any time I want to."

"I promise you…"

"It wasn't that way at all!"

"I'm not hurting anyone."

"It won't happen again."

"I only had a couple of beers."

"You're exaggerating!"

"What's the harm?"

"It's just between us, okay?"

"Don't tell!"

"———made me do it." (Usually another family member or a family problem gets the blame.)

Addiction almost always causes other family members to become codependents because they feel it is their responsibility to:

- Keep the family member's problem in the family, or . . .
- Deny there is a problem, or . . .
- Believe the addict's promises, or all of the above.

This is easy to understand. The drinking or drug-abusing person can embarrass the family. The other members pull together because they really love the dysfunctional member. But if you are raised in this situation, you come to believe that *all* families work this way, that *every* family goes through crisis after crisis. This, however, is not true.

Dan was disappointed. Once again, Dad hadn't come out to see him play center field. He checked the stands, lost his concentration

16 | *for a second, and nearly got beaned by a ball he should have caught. "I didn't think he'd show," Dan thought.*

Maybe it was better, after all. The last time Dad had come out, he was drunk, loud and obnoxious in the stands. Before the game ended, a neighbor had to walk him home. Dan's team won, but he didn't go out for sodas and burgers with his teammates afterward. He was too mad at Dad and too embarrassed by his behavior.

Why was Dad that way? When he drank, he often told Dan, "You can't do anything right." Maybe if he got better grades, Dan thought, Dad wouldn't get drunk so much.

Dan decided not to mention his father's drinking when he got home. He buttoned up his hurt and walked home from the field.

Addiction Always Upsets Family Balance

Addicts often claim that it is a problem within the family that makes them drink or do drugs. Sometimes there are other problems they can use as an excuse. But people with an addiction will do what they can do even if there are no other problems. They are unable to stop themselves until they recognize their addiction and seek help.

They do not react to a family

Alcoholics may reach for a drink first thing in the morning, or they may drink only on weekends.

problem—they *become* the family problem.

Problems with drug and alcohol abuse can upset the balance of the family. They can also cause codependency because they may:

- Entangle the family with the law (fights, auto accidents, drug possession)
- Embarrass other family members, which is a common reason for denying that the problem exists, and also for helping the addict feed his addiction
- Create instability within the family because of the drug user's unpredictable behavior

Alcohol is a legal and socially acceptable drug.

- Create distrust by breaking promises
- Distract the family from what its other members need by becoming the center of attention.

Janine's math final is tomorrow. Her mom promised to help her study tonight. Now, she can't: Aunt Ruth is off drinking again. Janine's mother had to leave and go find her sister. Janine is trying to study, but she knows she'll fail her test. She is angry.

"Why doesn't Aunt Ruth move somewhere else and take care of herself?" she thinks to herself. Then she feels guilty for thinking it.

What Janine doesn't know is that she's |
right! Aunt Ruth is someone to be sorry
for, but that doesn't mean she has to
mess up *other* lives.

Drug Addiction Includes Alcohol

Any addiction is disruptive, and a gambling addiction can ruin family finances.
But drug addiction is the most destructive. (A drug is any substance that can
change the way you feel, react, or see
things. You can easily overdose, with bad
results.)

Addicts almost always deny their
addiction. Sometimes they try to change,
but usually they can't. In addiction, the
body demands satisfaction. The addiction
takes control of the addict.

Although many people don't think of it
this way, alcohol is a drug. It can be highly
addictive for some people. It is the most
popular of all drugs for many reasons:

- Alcohol is legal for adults and is easy
  to get. It is sold in stores and (in
  many states) in supermarkets.
- Legal alcohol is of good quality.
  Unlike street drugs, it is considered
  "safe."
- Alcohol is socially acceptable. It is

20

served in bars and restaurants and at parties. It is heavily advertised, always as part of fun and good times. Also, many people don't think of beer or wine as "drinking." They don't believe that a beer drinker can be an alcoholic.

- Someone can be a genuine alcoholic and not drink every day. This kind of drinker is like a drug user. He or she can create codependency by keeping other family members off balance. They wonder when the next problem will arise, and what form it will take.

Substance Abuse Means Personality Changes

Eating disorders and gambling and spending addictions can all create codependency. But substance addictions create two problems: codependency among the family members and a personality change in the addict. The personality of an addict may change under the influence of alcohol, hard drugs, or misused prescription drugs. Such changes make a bad situation worse.

- The user behaves unpredictably. Moods may change from happy to depressed, kindly to abusive, easygoing to aggressive, agreeable to

Even shopping can become an addiction.

argumentative, loving to hostile. But *the same changes may not occur every time*. The family never knows how things will go.

- Commitments are forgotten and foolish promises made when the altered personality takes charge.
- The user can misbehave or be a danger, embarrassing the family and causing problems in public places or with the law.
- Addiction can trigger anger and abuse at home, with words, actions, or both.
- The addict becomes careless with

22

money he or she does not have or misspends it under the influence.
- The addict's unstable actions may cause a crisis at any moment without warning.

After the bad time is over, things may seem okay, but they aren't. The addicted person:

- Promises to shape up. He or she often knows from experience just what kinds of promises the codependent "doormats" will accept.
- Appears genuinely remorseful. The "doormats" want to believe "it won't happen again."
- May withdraw or become depressed in either a genuine or staged bid for codependents' sympathy.
- Breaks the promises made by repeating the problem behavior.

The codependents' big mistakes are thinking that they can change the things the troublesome family member does, and believing that by giving in (being codependent) they will improve the situation.

It's worth repeating the facts: Most

codependents don't realize that they *are* codependent. They honestly believe they are doing their duty by "helping" a troubled member of the family.

23

Try to believe:
1) *It's not your problem.*
2) *It's not your fault.*

That is easier said than done!

CHAPTER 2

How Does Compulsion Create Codependency?

*T*he great Russian writer Leo Tolstoy wrote in his famous novel *Anna Karenina*: "All happy families resemble one another, but each unhappy family is unhappy in its own way." In codependent families, addictive substances are not the only causes of dysfunction.

One cause of dysfunction (and often codependency) is an almost addictive compulsion to argue. Substance abuse can makes this tendency even worse. Constant disagreements arise among some adults about almost anything that strikes them wrong—money, young family members' dating hours, choice of friends, grades, spouse's working hours, even pets or other frictions.

Arguments often arise in a codependent family.

Other family members "handle" this fighting by avoiding it or by other codependent actions. They, in turn, often teach their children codependent behavior.

When she came home from school, Gloria walked in to see her mother's pinched face as she tried desperately not to yell back at whomever she was talking to on the phone, probably her husband. At last, she slammed down the phone, and, ignoring Gloria, went into her bedroom, and closed the door firmly.

"Great," Gloria thought. "Mom's trying to avoid an argument again. That means she'll

25

As a codependent, you may find yourself dealing with the situation by trying to be perfect.

avoid all of us too. I guess I'll have to get dinner ready." She reached into the refrigerator for some chicken and salad fixings. "I hate it when Mom gets like this. She stays silent until whomever she is angry with apologizes. But everyone feels how angry she is, no matter who it is or what it's about. She didn't talk to me for a week after I brought Mercedes home, with her pierced navel and nose. It took me days just to figure out why Mom was mad, and even longer to explain why Mercedes is so great."

When Gloria's mother was a child, her parents fought constantly. Her father drank a lot, which was usually what the arguments were about. Without knowing it, Gloria's mother became codependent. She tried—and failed—to stop the fighting. When she married, she said, "Never again," and vowed not to argue with her husband. But as a codependent, she still had a compulsion to control—to "keep the family in line" and to avoid arguments at any cost. Now, Mom manipulates her husband and daughter with her suspicions and her silences.

Like most codependents, Gloria and her father blame themselves on some level for Mom's constant silences. They both try to avoid the problem in their own ways. They would never talk about it with Mom, and they don't mention it to each other. Each member of this dysfunctional family lives behind a wall of silence and denial.

How Codependents Cope

Maybe Gloria's family sounds like yours, but in your case, drugs or alcohol use may play a day-to-day role. They may cause violent arguments, physical or verbal abuse, problems with strangers, or trouble with the police. Your problem, then, is even harder than Gloria's. You have drugs to cope with as well. Your codependent defenses may be

28 stronger than hers. You may do more than just tiptoe around someone's behavior.

When compulsion and addiction cause codependency, the codependents develop strong coping techniques. (If some coping methods sound just the opposite of others, remember that codependents try to cope with their dysfunctional family members and with their own lives in any way they think will work.)

If you are a codependent, you may (or may not):

- **Accept the blame.** This is the "It's all my fault" defense. You may honestly think that you are part of the problem, or you may have been told so by the problem person. You may play "doormat" to avoid an argument. In time, the blame idea takes hold. You truly believe it—and your self-esteem drops.
- **Try to be perfect.** This goes right along with accepting blame. You may believe that if you get top grades, make the ball team, keep the home clean, cook dinner every night, or find a new friend the family really likes, the home situation will improve. So you try to be perfect. Since nobody *is*

Codependents may also cope by trying to control people, especially the addict.

perfect, you feel rotten every time you think you've screwed up (like getting a C on your report card). Kids at school may call you a "goody-goody."

- **Deny the problem.** Denial is a big part of codependency—trying to pretend the problem doesn't exist or that you can make it go away. The problem person plays right along. He or she persuades you and others that what goes on in the family isn't anyone else's business. So you don't tell. You keep it bottled up.

- **Play for laughs.** You may use

30

humor and pretend to look on the bright side. You may even make jokes about what's going wrong. You may see this as your duty. Inside, you may be hurting, but you're denying the reality of the problem by trying to get everyone to laugh it off (a form of control).

- **Go along.** You may seem to agree with what everyone else wants to do, especially your friends. Secretly you hope to be accepted. But you hate to admit that what others want to do isn't what *you* want to do. Your self-appointed role is "people-pleaser." You deny what *you* want.
- **"Enable."** This word means "help something to happen." You and others may enable the problem person to misbehave by covering up for absences from work. Telephoning for a "sick" parent is not uncommon. Other enabling steps include cleaning up the destruction, or even buying drugs or alcohol. (A codependent may even go out drinking with an alcoholic relative to try to control what happens—but that is *really* "enabling.") Believing the problem person's promises is another form of

enabling. This paves the way for the
crisis to happen again. You can also
enable by doing nothing to help
yourself, or by believing that you
have to take the situation lying
down.

- **Clam up.** The codependent often
feels that there's no one to listen, so
what's the use of sharing? This is
not simply feeling sorry for yourself,
although many codependents do.
Everybody focuses on the problem
person—even you! So you may really
have no one to lean on. By clamming
up, you and others keep news of the
problem from spreading. You also
may prevent a confrontation, the one
thing you as a codependent want to
avoid. And locking up your own
thoughts is the safest way to get
by.
- **Control.** You may find that you're
trying hard to control others (such as
the problem person). However, you're
losing control over what you need and
what you feel. You may try to control
family and friends. You may even gain
attention by causing yourself to feel
sick. It isn't hard to do—but it's the
wrong control.

32 | ## *Troubles with Friends*

If you think you are a codependent to another family member's arguments, addictions, or compulsions, you may wish to reach outside your family and make more friends. This is not easy. You may know a lot of people your age but think not many of them like you. Instead of thinking positively about yourself and your friends, your difficult home situation probably has you thinking negatively.

So you tend to go along with what your friends want to do. You agree, even if what your friends want to do is dangerous. You think that if you go along, they'll like you better.

Or you may try to control friendships by saying things like, "If you liked me, you'd do this with me." Or you may put your friend on the defensive by saying, "You should *understand* how I feel." (Of course, you say this when you have not told your friend what you're truly thinking!)

Without realizing it, you may be playing communications tricks on your friends. You may make them do what you want by getting them to feel sorry for you. Or, if a friend really *does* want to do something friendly, you may be afraid he or she is getting too close: "You don't *really* want to do that. You're only suggesting it because you feel sorry for me."

The Hidden Dangers

You might think that, because you mostly go along with others and put yourself aside, being codependent is okay.

But it is not the best way for you to live. Denying your own feelings and needs is unhealthy. It is important to take care of yourself.

One day you may feel that you've had enough. You'll resent the way you have to act at home. You'll grow tired of being afraid to bring your friends to the house, or of feeling ashamed of your mother's pill-popping—or whatever the real problem is.

You'll give up. You'll stop trying to please everyone.

That is when one hidden danger may emerge.

Alone or with friends, you may see "a couple of beers" or "a toke now and then" as a way to sidestep family stress and problems for a few hours.

Your experiments may make things cool for a while—if you don't get caught.

34 | But there's a letdown after every high. And there are more hidden dangers.

For one thing, you may find that you can't manage liquor, pot, or other drugs. Everybody believes they can, but many people can't. About 10 percent of drinkers become alcoholics, and many of them grew up as codependent children in alcoholic families. Most alcoholics cannot free themselves of the hold that alcohol has on them without professional help or a support group such as Alcoholics Anonymous. Hard drug users, prescription drug abusers, and diet pill addicts have an even harder time getting clean.

If you got hooked, you would truly *become* the problem you wrongly thought you were all along! And codependents *do* tend to become substance users and abusers.

Even if you don't use liquor or drugs, being a codependent can become its own compulsion—the other danger. You grow so used to this unhealthy behavior that you honestly think it's normal. It takes on a life of its own.

CHAPTER 3

What Codependency Can Do to You

*C*odependency doesn't just happen. People *learn* it from living in unhealthy situations. Since they usually don't know they're codependent, such people do not realize they are learning unhealthy responses. But they are.

Codependents Live for Others

Codependents live *outside* their own lives. As Anne Wilson Schaef writes, "Codependents are totally dependent on others for their very right to exist." In a family trying to cope with one member's drug or alcohol problem, it's hard *not* to become a codependent. (Alcoholics Anonymous has a saying: *"Alcoholics do not have relationships—they take hostages."*)

Coping with others' problems can make you physically ill.

Rita really likes Alfredo, but she isn't sure he likes her. They often "happen" to meet after school and walk to his home (Rita knows just when Alfredo's basketball practice ends). Rita hopes Alfredo will ask her for a date, but he hasn't yet. She thinks maybe she isn't good enough for him.

"You've met my mom," Alfredo said to Rita on one of their walks, "but I've never met yours. Let's walk to your house today."

Rita panicked. It was 4:30, and she figured her mother would be half drunk. They would walk in on the smell of gin and breath mints—and goodness knows how **36** *Mom would react to a strange boy.*

"No," she lied. "My mom won't be home |
till late, and it wouldn't be right if you came
in the house. Our nosy next-door neighbor
would tell Mom, and then she'd get on my
case."

Alfredo looked disappointed, but he
agreed. When they said goodbye at his front
door, he didn't ask her to visit. She felt hurt,
but relieved, too. He could never meet Mom—
at least, not until Rita had gotten her to stop
drinking.

Yes, it would be hard for Rita to admit the truth about her home life. Weren't she, her dad, and her big brother silently trying to "manage" Mom's drinking? Wouldn't Rita feel ashamed if her mother said something off-the-wall to Alfredo? Wouldn't he be turned off if he knew her mother drank? Wasn't it her job to cover up for Mom by lying? It would keep her from being shamed by her mother's behavior.

Her family life has Rita so unsure of herself that she won't do anything to rock the boat. She puts aside her wishes so she can "do the right thing" for Mom, even though Mom is not doing the right thing for Rita or the rest of the family. Rita is the "perfect" codependent.

38

Rita's codependency makes her a controlling person, too. She controlled what she saw might be a damaging situation by lying and inventing a "nosy neighbor." She sees controlling Mom's drinking as her job. What she wants to do for herself doesn't count. She doesn't think she's worth much, anyway.

These are perfect examples of what codependency can do to someone. Are *you* one of those "someones"?

An Alphabetical Codependent List

Rita's example, and the other cases and situations you've read about, give you an idea of what codependency can do. This list will tell you more.

The first step in recovering from codependency is being *aware* of what codependents feel and how they act. Like the other traits you've read about, many of these things will be opposites of one another.

Codependents can be (but are not always):

- **Agreeable.** They agree with others' decisions just to keep peace, or because they think their ideas don't count.

- **Angry.** They may not show it, but
  they resent always giving in. Their
  buried anger will show up later.
- **Caretakers.** They see helping
  the problem person as their duty.
- **Compulsive.** They are always
  focused on the problem person. They
  frequently talk about him or her—
  and other people. They may easily
  become addicted to substances or
  bad habits.
- **Controlling.** This is the trademark
  of codependents. They try to control
  everything: the problem person, their
  friends, their feelings, others' needs.
- **Crisis-prone.** Some codependents
  thrive on crisis because it gives them
  something to control. Sometimes
  they create a crisis to gain attention.
- **Denying.** Another trademark. They
  deny the problem, deny their own
  needs, deny their self-worth.
- **Difficult.** Some codependents create
  problems to gain attention or in re-
  venge for others' bad actions.
- **Distrustful.** They learn not to trust
  the problem person. Distrust of
  others grows from there. This is a
  major codependent problem.
- **Enabling.** They may help the prob-

Codependents sometimes find that they feel depressed.

lem person continue the problem actions as a way of gaining control or of keeping things secret.

- **Failure-prone.** Codependents' lack of self-esteem makes them blame themselves for others' failures, believe they can do nothing right, and feel they're not good enough. Codependents often team up with losers in destructive relationships.
- **Fearful.** The fear is real. Living with a difficult person creates a constant dread. Codependents are afraid to talk about the real family situation. They also fear rejection by friends.

They push friends away by being afraid to trust, and thus earn the rejection they fear.

- **Giving.** They feel safest when giving, not getting. This includes going along with others' wishes even when these are not right for them.
- **Guilt-ridden.** Codependents feel guilty about feeling okay about themselves, and especially about receiving help from others.
- **Helpless, indecisive.** Helplessness may be a crutch to get attention—or codependents may truly feel unable to cope with their situation or make a decision.
- **Humorous.** False humor is often used to get through bad times. They exert control by trying to get others to laugh.
- **Irresponsible** for themselves, since they are so busy being responsible for others.
- **Low on self-esteem.** They accept blame for everything, including others' failures. They believe they are no good.
- **Manipulative.** Getting people to do things their way is controlling the situation.

42

- **Neglectful.** Codependents usually neglect their own needs. They also neglect grades, appearances, and their inner selves. After all, who cares?
- **Overreacting.** Codependents often overreact even to slight criticism or blame. They do not believe compliments or praise.
- **Perfect.** Codependents expect to be perfect. They think their perfect behavior will do away with the family's problems.
- **Physically ill.** Dealing with their own emotions and others' problems can cause genuine sickness.
- **Rescuing.** Their mission in life is to rescue others, especially the family's problem person. They will probably go through life trying to rescue everyone.
- **Repressed.** They keep everything bottled up inside—it's safer that way.
- **Self-centered.** Even though their lives are given over to serving others, the codependents' world revolves around their own troubles.
- **Self-pitying.** When their noble efforts fail to change others, they feel sorry for themselves. Codependents

make great martyrs—always sacrific-
ing for others.

- **Shameful.** They feel ashamed of
their families, their own supposed
failures, and their inability to improve things by controlling them.
- **Suicidal.** Codependents may feel
this way if they stay codependent
long enough and don't get help.
- **Uncommunicative, withdrawn.**
They believe that the less they say,
the less trouble they'll have; the less
they share, the less they'll be hurt.

If you see yourself in this list (and are
not denying that you do!), you have become *aware*. Awareness is the first step in
getting unhooked from codependency.

The second step is *accepting* the truth
that you are codependent. There is no
shame in being a codependent—your
family situation has made you one. If you
accept that fact, you will begin to understand many things in different ways.

It won't be easy.

It *will* be worth it!

How to Start Your Life Over

*O*nce you realize you are codependent, you will have to make moves to help yourself. You do *not* make these moves alone. The job is too big for that. You will need to reach out for help (we'll come to that later).

But even when you get help, you are the one who has to do the work. It will involve changing the way you *think* about addiction, about trust, about coping, about family members and—most important of all—about yourself.

All this will take time. That's okay. After all, it took years for you to become codependent.

As you change your thinking, you will

work through some tough times. But

There are many people you can reach out to for help, including a favorite teacher.

once you are there, you will be on top of life. It won't be on top of you.

Think About Addiction in a Different Way

If the addiction of a family member is at the heart of your codependence, addiction is the first item to sit down and think about realistically.

You must realize that nothing you do or don't do will change the addicted person. Only something *he or she* does to change bad habits and attitudes has any chance of working.

This is hard to accept. After all,

46 haven't you (and other family members) been "helping" by trying to control the addict and get him or her to change? It hasn't worked, but it might succeed next time? On the contrary, only when an addict admits being powerless over the situation and seeks help *without being pushed by others* is there any hope of improvement.

Once you see that you can do nothing to change the drug-affected person, you have to accept the next truth: that you are not responsible for their choices and behavior.

However, you are responsible for your own actions. If you have done bad things to get even because you feel hurt by the family member's actions, those actions are your responsibility. This approach probably hasn't helped anybody anyway, including you.

The person you have to change is not the addict.

It's you.

Think About Trust in a Different Way

You want to believe the addict's promises. Then, if they are kept, you as a controlling codependent can take credit for the improvement. But time after time, the

addict lets you down. You may still hope,
but you no longer *trust.*

Okay, so you can't trust the addict. But that doesn't mean you cannot trust *anyone.* Other older people, or even a good friend, can be trusted.

The first step in getting help is to find a responsible adult or friend you can talk to. It might be a teacher or coach, your guidance counselor, or a minister, priest, or rabbi. You could choose a relative who is outside the immediate family. Maybe the parents of a school friend could help you, or an older friend of your family who knows your situation.

Ralph liked his auto mechanics class. It was a great mix of using tools to fix cars and learning the technical side such as computerized engine diagnosis. "Once I figure something out in class, it doesn't change," he thought. "A lot different from home!"

Mr. Nesbitt, his teacher, praised Ralph's progress—something his father never did. When his Dad did a line and got high, he'd drive Ralph nuts about going to college, mostly because he never went. Ralph just couldn't talk to Dad.

He found he could talk to Mr. Nesbitt. In fact, it was his teacher who asked him one

The problems in the life of a codependent can seem over-whelming.

day if he had anything on his mind he wanted to talk about.

"How did you know?" Ralph asked.

"It doesn't take rocket science to figure it out," Mr. Nesbitt said. "You're good with cars, and you're going to make a fine mechanic—but some days I can see you're down. You don't seem to grasp things I know you can learn. Is there something I can help you with?"

Nobody had ever asked Ralph what they could do for him! He was surprised and suspicious. But Mr. Nesbitt wasn't putting him down. He really did want to help.

48 *Little by little, Ralph came to understand*

that he could trust his teacher. Mr. Nesbitt didn't push him to talk, but whenever things got too bad with his father's drug-taking, he "unloaded" on Mr. Nesbitt.

Later, Ralph got into a self-help program at Mr. Nesbitt's suggestion. After graduation, they kept in touch. Ralph never forgot how he had learned to trust by talking over his problems with the auto mechanics teacher.

Ralph was lucky: Mr. Nesbitt asked the right questions. But you shouldn't wait for someone to come to you. Make your own move.

Think About Coping in a Different Way

You don't need to learn to cope—codependents always cope, but in the wrong ways. You *do* need to learn to cope positively, not negatively.

The first, most important, and *hardest* thing to think about is this: Stop trying to control situations that are out of your hands and not your fault.

To do this, you need to develop a coping technique called *detachment*. Not the kind of detachment that makes you hide in your room to avoid a problem, but

50 the kind that lets you step back in your mind from others' problems. It's a form of letting go.

Letting go is hard. Patti Davis, daughter of former President Reagan, writes in *The Way I See It*, "You think that, next time, [the situation] will be different. You don't return [to the family] for punishment, you return for love." But punishment is what you may get.

That is what makes letting go hard to do. You may not like your mother or father when they're caught up in their drug or alcohol use—but you still *love* them because they're your parents. It's the *love* that makes you a codependent, trying to solve their problem.

You should try to love the addict, but if you can't that's okay, too. The addict really hates himself or herself when drugs or alcohol are in command. This hatred and feeling of insecurity may lead to the addiction.

You have to start respecting yourself, thinking you are a good, strong person. If you're angry, direct that anger at the addiction, not the addict. Stop accepting blame for the addict's problems, even though he or she may blame you. That, too, is part of detachment.

Keeping a journal is often helpful in sorting out your feelings.

52 Here are other coping steps you should take:

- **Start keeping a journal or diary.**
  Writing down what happens, what you
  think, and how you feel about it will
  help you cope more positively as you
  work at letting go and at developing
  new ways to think. Later, you may
  want to share these thoughts with
  someone you trust and who is trained
  to help (but you don't have to). Or as
  time passes, you can review earlier
  entries to see how your thinking is
  changing.
- **Develop a "Plan B" for you and
  any younger children** in your
  family to use when the drug or
  alcohol scene gets out of hand.
  Plan ahead with a trusted friend or
  neighbor so that you have a place to
  go when trouble strikes. Your plan
  should include calling the police if
  the situation gets really dangerous.
  To do this, you'll have to be strong
  enough to take the family's blame for
  the results.
- **Keep cool.** Try to stay apart from the
  action, instead of making things worse
  in efforts to control the situation.

- **Stay straight yourself.** You can't do the hard thinking and make the changes you must in your life if you're messing up your head with drugs or liquor.
- **Join a support group.** Even if you have a friend you can trust, this is a vital step. People in support groups are *trained* to help you start thinking positively about yourself.

Think About Yourself in a Different Way

In their introductory booklet *"Is CoDA-Teen for Me?"*, Co-Dependents Anonymous addresses people aged 13 through 19 with these comments, among others:

". . . Some [relationships] may seem more difficult than others. We often encounter mixed messages from our friends and families that can leave us feeling lonely, confused, frustrated, and angry.

"In CoDA-Teen, there is a safe place to go and tell how we feel, without being criticized, judged, or given advice. CoDA-Teen is a closed meeting for teenagers. Hosts offer silent support.

"The benefits of the fellowship are many. You begin to believe in a Higher

54 Power of your own understanding, believe in yourself and your judgment, and trust other teens. You learn to trust in 'the process' of recovery, and know that you deserve healthy, loving relationships for the rest of your life."

Like Co-Dependents Anonymous for adults, CoDA-Teen is a program based on the 12 steps to recovery first developed by Alcoholics Anonymous. A self-help group such as CoDA-Teen or Alateen (an Alcoholics Anonymous group for children of alcoholic parents) will help you think about yourself in a more positive way.

Work Through the Five Steps

Whether you are part of a self-help group or talking to a trusted friend, you will have to work through these five stages to get unhooked from codependence. If you think positively about yourself and recognize each step, it will be easier than if you resist them.

- **Denial.** Recovering codependents may still want to deny there's a problem. Admitting there is one is the first step to recovery.
- **Anger.** It's natural to be angry about

It can be tempting to turn to drugs for relief.

56

what others have done to you—and what you have let them do. You will have to work through this. It's okay to hate what happened, but try not to go on hating the people involved.

- **Sadness.** When the anger wears off, you may feel sad about all the unhappy times in your childhood. It's hard not to replay the past, slipping back into anger. This, too, is something you have to work your way through.
- **Apathy.** Apathetic people feel knocked out. You may, too, after you've gone through the emotional roller-coaster ride of denial, anger, and sadness. Spend quiet time. Don't rush. You will work through this stage, too, once you recognize it.
- **Acceptance.** You will finally realize that you can't change your childhood. It's time to stop clinging to the past. When you do, *the bad times will lose their power to control your thinking.* You can truly begin to think differently about yourself, and about those around you.

Set Your Boundaries
Once you are thinking positively about

yourself, the time will come when you're strong enough to set boundaries. Those are the limits of what you will accept from others and from yourself. Your boundaries may include not allowing yourself to be verbally abused, be put down, or physically abused, or not enabling the addict. You may have to be strong to make others see your boundaries. You will have to be strong with yourself, too, to avoid slipping back into codependent habits.

The final step toward recovery will be your ability to be not independent but *interdependent*. This means living in a balance of fairness, with easily understood give-and-take between you and other family members and friends.

Don't become discouraged. All this will take time. You may take one step backward for every two steps forward. That's all right. You can—and will—come out ahead.

Glossary
Explaining New Words

addiction Any compulsive behavior that
a person cannot control.

alcohol The drug found in beer, liquor,
and wine. Alcohol affects behavior and
is often addictive.

behavior How a person acts; what he or
she does.

boundary The acceptable limits you
impose on your behavior toward others
and on their behavior toward you.

codependent Someone who tries to
control another person's behavior and
who cannot keep up good relationships.

compulsion Any uncontrollable

behavior. (Codependency can become a compulsion.)

control   Getting someone to do what you want; attempting to direct another person's actions.

denial   Not admitting that a problem exists.

dependency   Inability to do without a substance or a method of behavior.

detachment   The process of separating yourself from the problems of an addict or compulsive person.

drug   Any substance that, if misused, can negatively affect the way a person thinks or acts. Very often addictive.

dysfunctional family   One that cannot meet its members' needs in a positive way.

interdependence   A balanced, normal relationship in which give and take are equal.

manipulation   See *control*.

self-help group   Group of people who meet together to help each other deal with a problem they share, often with leaders trained to help.

Help List

Turn first to your guidance counselor, school psychologist, a trusted adult, or a minister, priest, or rabbi. Also, look in your telephone book for Alcoholism Information and Treatment Centers, Drug Abuse and Addiction Information and Treatment, Crisis Intervention Services, Mental Health Agencies, and Self-Help Groups. Look in your local newspaper for meeting places and times for one or more of the self-help groups below, or write or call for information.

AGENCIES AND GROUPS

Adult Children of Alcoholics
P.O. Box 35623
Los Angeles, CA 90035

Al-Anon/Alateen
Box 862, Midtown Station
New York, NY 10018-6106

**Co-Dependents Anonymous/
  CoDA-Teen**
P.O. Box 33577
Phoenix, AZ 85067-3577

Daughters and Sons United
P.O. Box 952
San Jose, CA 95108-0952

Families Anonymous
P.O. Box 528
Van Nuys, CA 91408

Narcotics Anonymous
16155 Wyandotte Street
Van Nuys, CA 91406

**National Association for Children of
Alcoholics**
31706 Pacific Coast Highway
South Laguna, CA 95677

HOTLINES (TOLL-FREE CALLS)

Cocaine hotline
1-800-COCAINE

National Adolescent Suicide Hotline
1-800-621-4000

**National Council on Alcoholism
hotline**
1-800-NCA-CALL

**National Institute on Drug Abuse
(NIDA) Drug-Referral Hotline**
1-800-662-HELP

For Further Reading

Beattie, Melody. *Codependent No More.*
San Francisco: Harper/Hazelden,
1987.

Black, Claudia. *It Will Never Happen to
Me: Children of Alcoholics.* New York:
Ballantine Books, 1991.

Davis, Patti. *The Way I See It.* New York:
G. B. Putnam's Sons, 1992; Jove
paperback ed., 1993.

McFarland, Rhoda. *Drugs and Your Parents.* New York: Rosen Publishing
Group, 1991.

Porterfield, Kay Marie. *Coping with
Codependency,* rev. ed. New York:
Rosen Publishing Group, 1994.

Schaef, Anne Wilson. *Co-Dependence;
Misunderstood—Mistreated.* San
Francisco: HarperCollins, 1986.

Septien, Al. *Everything You Need to Know
about Codependency.* New York: Rosen
Publishing Group, 1993.

Index

A

addiction
    acceptance of, 43, 56
    causing codependency, 12
Alateen, 54
alcohol addiction, 12–13,
    19–20
Alcoholics Anonymous, 34
anger
    in abuse, 21
    at addiction, 49
    in addiction, 21
    in codependency, 39,
    54–56
Anna Karenina, 24
apathy, 56
argue, compulsion to, 24, 27
awareness, of codependency,
    38, 43

B

Beattie, Melody, 9
behavior, unpredictable,
    20–21
blame
    accepting, 28–29
    rejecting, 49
boundaries, setting, 56–57

C

CoDA-Teen, 53–54
codependency
    acceptance of, 45
    in childhood, 26
    dangers of, 33–34
    defined, 7, 9
codependent, 7
    growing up in alcoholic
        family, 34
    living for others, 35–38
    self-blame of, 26
    self-neglact of, 42
    self-pity of, 42–43
Codependent No More, 9

Co-Dependents Anonymous,
    9, 23
compulsion, addiction as, 13,
    18, 39
confrontation, avoiding, 31
control, 38, 39
    compulsion to, 27
    losing, 31
    seeking and also having,
    9–10
coping methods,
    codependents', 27–31,
    48–53

D

Davis, Patti, 49
death, upsetting family
    balance, 10
denial of problem, 15, 19,
    27, 28, 29, 39, 54
depression, 22
detachment, 48
dieting addiction, 12–13
distraction from family needs,
    18
distrust, 18, 39
"doormat," playing, 28
drug addiction, 12–13, 19, 20

E

eating addiction, 12–13, 20
embarrassment by addict, 17
emergency plan, 52
enabling, 29, 39–40

F

family
    balance maintained, 12
    balance upset, 10
    by addiction, 1–17
    by drugs and alcohol, 17
    by fights, 25
    dysfunctional, 6, 10, 12, 27
    healthy, 6

64

fear, of addict's behavior, 17, 40–41
friends, troubles with, 32

G
gambling addiction, 12, 19, 20
guilt, feeling of, 41

H
helplessness, 41
humor, as coping method, 28–29, 41

I
illness, upsetting family balance, 10
interdependence, 57
Is CoDA-Teen for Me?, 53

J
job loss, upsetting family balance, 10
journal, keeping, 52

M
manipulation, 41
moving, as upsetting family balance, 10

P
people-pleaser, role as, 29

perfectionism, 28, 42
personality changes, 20–22
positive coping methods, 49
promises, broken, 15, 21, 22, 29, 46

R
remorse, addict's, 22
repression, 42

S
sadness, 56
Schaef, Anne Wilson, 35
self-blame, 10
self-esteem, loss of, 28, 38, 40, 41
self-respect, 50
silence, of dysfunctional family, 27
spending addiction, 12–13, 20
support, 34, 53

T
Tolstoy, Leo, 24
trust in friend, developing, 47

W
Way I See It, The, 49
withdrawal, 22, 30, 43

About the Authors

Mary Price Lee holds a B.A. in English and an M.S. in Education from the University of Pennsylvania. She is a former educator, now a free-lance writer. Richard S. Lee has an A.B. in English from The College of William and Mary. He is a career advertising writer and free-lance author. This is the Lees' twenty-first book, their tenth for the Rosen Publishing Group. The Lees also wrote Drugs and the Media and Caffeine and Nicotine for the Drug Abuse Prevention Library.

Photo Credits
Cover photo: by Michael Brandt
All other photos by Yung-Hee China